W9-CDM-836

Women Whose Lives Are Food,
Men Whose Lives Are Money

Women
Whose Lives
Are Food,

Other poetry volumes by Joyce Carol Oates

Anonymous Sins and Other Poems 1969
Love and Its Derangements 1970
Angel Fire 1973
The Fabulous Beasts 1975

Men
Whose Lives
Are Money

Poems by JOYCE CAROL OATES

Illustrated by Elizabeth Hansell

LOUISIANA STATE UNIVERSITY PRESS
Baton Rouge and London
1978

The poems published here have appeared previously in the following periodicals, sometimes in slightly different forms: *American Poetry Review, Boston University Journal, Brushfire, California Quarterly, Canadian Forum, Canadian Literature, Capilano Review, Concerning Poetry, Epoch, Georgia Review, Helios, Hudson Review, Kansas Quarterly, Little Magazine, Michigan Quarterly Review, Missouri Review, Modern Poetry Studies, Nation, New Republic, Niagara, Ohio Review, Ontario Review, Poem, Poetry Northwest, Prairie Schooner, Prism International, Quarry S C, Southern Review, Western Humanities Review, Windsor Review*.

A broadside of "Public Outcry" was published in a limited edition by the Slow Lorris Press.

To all these acknowledgment and thanks are due.

Designer: Albert Crochet
Type Face: VIP Palatino
Typesetter: Graphic World, Inc., St. Louis, Missouri
Printer and binder: Kingsport Press, Kingsport, Tennessee

LIBRARY OF CONGRESS CATALOGING IN PUBLICATION DATA

Oates, Joyce Carol, 1922–
    Women whose lives are food, men whose lives are money.

    I. Title.
PS3565.A8W62   811'.5'4   77–17220
ISBN 0–8071–0391–8

To my parents Caroline and Frederick

Contents

I

**Women Whose Lives Are Food,
Men Whose Lives Are Money**

Women Whose Lives Are Food,
Men Whose Lives Are Money

Mid-morning Monday she is staring
peaceful as the rain in that shallow back yard
she wears flannel bedroom slippers
she is sipping coffee
she is thinking—
                              —gazing at the weedy bumpy yard
at the faces beginning to take shape
in the wavy mud
in the linoleum
where floorboards assert themselves

Women whose lives are food
breaking eggs with care
scraping garbage from the plates
unpacking groceries hand over hand

Wednesday evening: he takes the cans out front
tough plastic with detachable lids
Thursday morning: the garbage truck whining at 7
Friday the shopping mall open till 9
bags of groceries unpacked
hand over certain hand

Men whose lives are money
time-and-a-half Saturdays
the lunchbag folded with care and brought back home
unfolded Monday morning

Women whose lives are food
because they are not punch-carded
because they are unclocked
sighing glad to be alone
staring into the yard, mid-morning
mid-week
by mid-afternoon everything is forgotten

There are long evenings
panel discussions on abortions, fashions, meaningful work
there are love scenes where people mouth passions
sprightly, handsome, silly, manic
in close-ups revealed ageless
the women whose lives are food
the men whose lives are money

fidget as these strangers embrace and weep and mis-
        understand and forgive and die and weep and embrace
and the viewers stare and fidget and sigh and
begin yawning around 10:30
never made it past midnight, even on Saturdays,
watching their brazen selves perform

Where are the promised revelations?
Why have they been shown so many times?
Long-limbed children a thousand miles to the west
hitch-hiking in spring, burnt bronze in summer
thumbs nagging
eyes pleading
Give us a ride, huh? Give us a ride?

and when they return nothing is changed
the linoleum looks older
the Hawaiian Chicken is new
the girls wash their hair more often
the boys skip over the puddles
in the GM parking lot
no one eyes them with envy

their mothers stoop
the oven doors settle with a thump
the dishes are rinsed and stacked and
by mid-morning the house is quiet
it is raining out back
or not raining
the relief of emptiness rains
simple, terrible, routine
at peace

Visionary Adventures of a Wild Dog Pack

Snow-stubbled January fields and evil
frozen between our toes
by the time you see us
it is already too late
we trot across the vegetable world
in a pack of mad teeth and tongues

Voices in you speak
to our furious sorrow
we hear nothing
we are worm-ridden
bullet-shy
starving-crafty
we lap at pools of Arctic cold
we devour garbage
teeth and tongues and rib-rippling sides

Look:
a pack of stomachs covered in snarled fur!

Once over-loved we are now displaced
last summer's pets abandoned
by the roadside
not even lonely now
but forgetful of our old names
grunting and whining and squealing
a pack of stomachs roused at dusk
tongues aslant in stained mouths

We look like laughter, don't we?
tearing these feathery things apart
flinging the blood into the air
we charge in a pack
we whine and dodge and flee
savage-sad
wise mouths and guts
over-leaping our pet names
over-leaping the love
of our masters

Hauled from River, Sunday 8 A.M.

Many-ringed fingers, you note,
and hair a sodden waist-length mass,
and o! my poor face that deserved kisses
so stormed upon!—
you who loved me would not know me now.

Awash this morning amid the hulks of freighters,
turning, bobbing in the thin chilly froth,
a god's vengeance has drained from every wound
and those eyes that maddened some are now mismatched—
like the shredded cheap clothes
and the silver chain tight-twisted
and the lip broken to swell like a frantic fat toad.

It was not the death I dreamt of
but I asked for it, you are whispering.
Such a storm of blows!—brought it onto myself.
Hadn't I known better, why had I provoked,
couldn't I have sensed how the soft down of my upper lip
would tease him to a frenzy—?
A girl, a victim.
Awash this morning in the Sabbath harbor
and the boardwalk strollers gathered round
in a shocked resentful ring.

Former Movie Queen, Dying of Cancer, Watches an Old Movie of Hers at a Film Festival in San Francisco

Ah, there.
The beauty of that face
stirs me as if it weren't
my own.

Look.
There.
The beauty of that
stirs me as if
it weren't
me.

Listen: words
they invented,
wire-knots tight,
tightly twisted,
causing her to sing.
How can she not sing?

Sing.

The body's supple trickery,
the perfect tight-stretched skin.
It performs, it dances.
It obeys the sacred text.
A miracle?
Me.

Look, she strides across the screen—

> Here, a silky rag tied tight,
> tight about the head.
> Hair fallen out in clumps,
> bald silly head, mine.
> Don't look.
> One eye milky, overflowing the socket.
> Feet leaden, arm heavy as stone
> but not dead: not!

Breasts, shoulders, belly,
gay swinging arms.

The world leaps back into place.
Look at her legs, so shrewd!
And the mockery of those young eyes!

She strides through the dreaming
nation, through the dreams
of angry lovers.
She is improvised, she is theirs.
Eternal, she is yours.

Ah, but the beauty of that face
the miracle of that
counterfeiting death now
the pulse of that, that
raw glowering life
a song that screams of joy
happiness pecking at the eyes—
No escape, she is filling every space,
she is everywhere you look—

> The theater's floor is deep in mud.
> The wheelchair seems to be stuck.
> Someone is weeping, no matter,
> someone is laughing, don't be shy,
> don't be morbid, someone signs
> autographs with left hand—
> wild affectionate scrawl—
> *Love & Kisses Forever!*

> The houselights glare up,
> the universe claps me into life.
> Eighty-seven pounds, head trembling
> on raddled neck, am I hers, am
> I yours?—theirs?

> Whose?

A pretty death.
In flashbacks, one embrace
and another,

and the sun-warmed wind
tearing them apart.
So soon!
And that loveless daylight
her beauty fades into!

> Here, the tedium of infinity.
> All is darkness, all is balance.
> No dancing, no raging, no hurt.
> The pain was hers, not mine.
> This mud is a tide
> no moon can quicken.

The Eternal Children

The children are fighting happily in the playground.
Is it mid-winter, is it spring, is it autumn again?
They are fighting in the playground and in the schoolyard
and on the sidewalk and in the street.
Cars sound their horns
when they fight in the street.
The children are scuffling and shouting and laughing.
You can see them at 10:15 and at 12:30 and again at 3.
They are fighting happily on the sidewalk
outside MacGregor's Variety Store.
They are fighting at the curb.
Some shout heartily, some emit tiny screams.
Some wipe their noses on their sleeves and grin.
Struck hard on the back, they cough hollowly and recover.
They recover at once.

The children are fighting in the playground
and in the schoolyard and on the sidewalk
and in the street.
They are never serious.
One of them by decree is uglier than the others.
If he is ugly, very well then: He is ugly.
If his skin is gray and pitted
if his eyes are soapstone
if he cringes rat-quick and cruel
and smiles that slow-breaking wide sly smile
unlocking tooth after tooth—
if he dances a murderer's jig
if his stare cuts through you
if his secret is *I can't feel your pain*
very well then: There he is.

He leads the fight in the alley by the hardware store.
His fists rise and fall like twin hammers.
His shouts are piercing in the vacant lot by the school
and in the snow-soiled wading pool
and in the A & P parking lot, among the cars.
Is it autumn, is it summer, is it mid-winter already?
The children are not serious. The children are eternal.
Their tears and their giggles are blown away by the wind.
He dives among them, triumphant.
Very well then, he cries: Here I am.

From the Dark Side of the Earth

Invisible creatures everywhere
    like thoughts
I must boil water, daily
So much writhing life here in Asia
daily I boil water

Daily the tree of radiance blossoms
tough in me: steely nerves & muscles aching
    to be displayed
a body you misjudged now pulses daily
I no longer beg for crumbs
I am now calculating our future

Regulations are posted
    WATER MUST BE BOILED BEFORE DRINKING
yet I would not boil away my hatred
precious
to me precious in exile
as the scattering of signs on my body

Unreadable to profane eyes!
unreadable to mocking eyes like yours
yet perfect as the constellation that swings
    now above your half of the Earth
    and now above mine

The small gift I sent did not explode
into your eyes
& was not meant to: only a warning
Tho' I am exiled on the dark side of the earth
& you are basking in the light, Joyce,
don't underestimate me.

A man's argument with a woman
is his argument with himself
& I have often raked my teeth
across my mirror-image
    groaning with rage

I hate you both
but would not lose you

II

Metamorphoses

Lovers Asleep

Half the continent sleeps between us.
Half the population has leapt into costume,
a cluster of selves that rolls our eyeballs
    to exhaustion. . . .
How strenuous we know it, the innocence of sleep!

Forbidden by the midwestern plains
to know each other, nevertheless
we drift into each other:
we overlap somewhere west of Kansas City—
sharing a costume, an angel to be thrown to earth,
the impulse of the abyss.

The Spectre

I am long-bodied
ethereal yet langorous
    bluish-pale my skin, like dough
limbs long   heavy with muscle   unresisting

my vision is cunning
beneath these drooping heavy lids
and the spread of my arms is legendary!—
    fingertips long and narrow and sharp as feathers

I fall to earth without protest
as if this were my dream and not yours
a spectre
unresisting as I fall
only a spectre
a woman, an angel, burdened with such a body
fleshy dough that breathes, boneless
only a dream-spectre

the dreamer awakens with a shriek
his cries deny me
    as I strike him and our weights double
    treble
    swell to annihilation

The Lovers

Locked in love as the sky to its mock color
in a frieze of love like beauty in ancient profile
the lovers are a blatant litany
the lovers are hoarse with shouting of each other
their zeal eyeless and terrible
their moods promiscuous
　　　　as shiny black flies

Locked in love like the glowing bodies of wrestlers
in a panic of love as God pushes from every pore
the lovers laugh shrilly
the lovers see nothing funny
locked in love they are immortal
they are writhing in pain

Unlocked they would be like us
like us faintly quizzical
full-faced and glad of borders, walls,
　　　　ceilings, sills,
margins and boundaries and floors
and knowing what we are not

Locked in love they are tortured by Furies
　　　　of thought:
Should one fail, what would the other do?
Should one lose faith, how would the other survive?
Mere death would canonize them
it is not mere death they fear

it is not mere death they fear

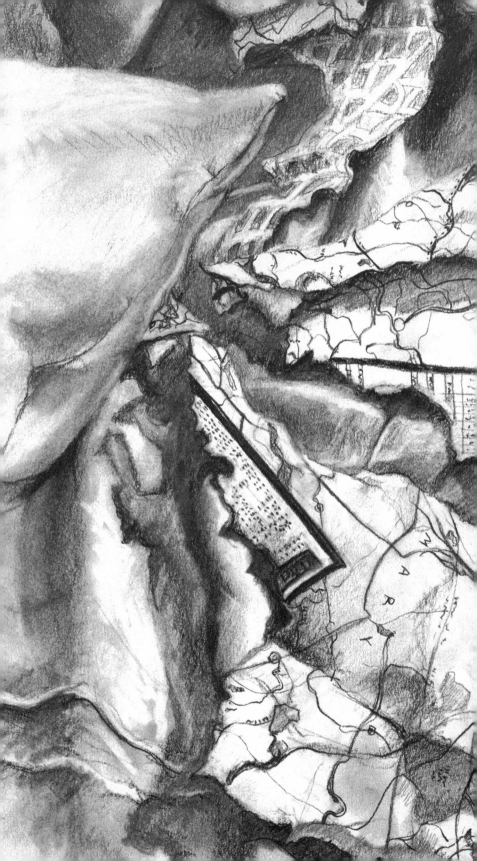

Fever Song

About the room flames breathe lightly
someone's arms are heavy around your neck
the sockets of your eyes are hot with shadow
O love is the cry pulling you down
Love the arms weigh

Are you dying so easily, a slattern?
and no protest?

Orangy-hot as a child's taste of ether
is your own fetid breath
you are no longer who, you are what
lazy and slippery
the love-pulse gone wild

No: you are a flat map opened wide
every direction squeezed into a single point

Overhead is something great-winged
and fiery of breath
as a Russian seraph
something enormously mute
as the sea quaking orange flame

Tonight the full moon will strike
it will be the Resurrection
but you will see nothing
your eyelids are opaque
at the center of your pulse is a counting
splendid as a tree aching with fruit
pulp and seed and peel:
miracle

You wake: St. George in bronze robes tramples
a dog-sized dragon:
its scaly tongue protrudes
in thirst and defeat

You run lightly about the room   about the walls
your hair flames orange
your laughter is triumphant as stained glass
you wake from the grave of bedsheets:
a miracle

Addiction

Always this hunger
    this perfect thirst
Always a gusty wind!—
    the flags fly
    the sailboats race
Always the drama of snow always the spillage of sun
always the chiming of the hour always the perfect hand
dealt to you always that crunching of the gravel
as Fate draws near

        There are other times. They are not this time.
        This is the only time.

Always this hunger
    this perfect thirst
Turn the knob and the image appears it is yours!
Lift the receiver and the voice leaps forth it is yours!

The air snaps with tiny kisses
the Christmas ornaments are big enough to ride
always perfect calm and every hair in place
always a bracing wind and the edge of the world in sight!

        What had you done with your life before this?

Last Harvest

That last harvest the cornfields were paved
the newts were translated to jets' keening wails
everywhere I stumbled I turned to look back
everywhere creatures froze cunning as stone

A sweep of my massive hand crushed a city
and the winds rushed together like a knot
when I snorted with laughter
innocent as a gale

That last harvest the bubble of a globe
floated weightless into the night
yawning I felt something tug at my eyelids
I felt gravity itself turning to ice

I sickened and lay across continents
my fingers scooped waves of sand
my great head went hollow with grief
losing one by one the sacred words
of harvest, gale, bubble, grief, globe

Holy Saturday

for Milton White

The imperial city was heaped with broken concrete
we tried all night to piece together again
blinded by the glare of headlights from cars and vans
our timid fingers minutely stung

In play men of the city carried their smaller companions high
in play they threw them down onto the rubble
we unloosed fire-bright sirens, we consulted our maps
the web of stars overhead had begun to fray

Intoxicated with pride the great Schopenhauer was flown about
in a Detroit police helicopter
"Here—and here—and here also! And *here*"
he shouted above the heaving streets

The night was snarled and immense and pocked with tiny lights
and I do not think we have come to the end
for our heads reel like cracked crockery
and the stench of oil is on our clothes

and at midnight one of the children
shot his younger brother dead
with a .22 rifle of his father's
and again we unloosed sirens, we flattened our wrinkled maps

> Once day came we could of course rejoice
> in tulips delicate as the streaked shells
> of painted Easter eggs—
> and the Bell Tower on the green
> stroke by stroke defining its noble art
> against an eager country silence

Skyscape

The entire morning drew my gaze
I saw no one I knew
not clouds but human shapes
a battalion of statues darkening the sky

These were presences to weigh harshly
against the unprotected eye
but there was no harm to them
no terror to their infinite calm

I saw no one I knew

I saw everyone:
men who were granite columns,
women in an ecstasy of white marble,
children dwarfed by seraphims' wings

Stately and inhuman as clouds
white and smooth and perfect
all those stony brows
those egg-like sightless eyes

Their muscled flesh is prodigious
and uncontaminated by the heat of our blood
warriors, gargoyles, horses, women
who have borne stone children out of their stony loins

Oblivious of our worship and our dread
they pass in their methodical calm
they are ruthless in beauty
massive, perfect, moon-pale, merely rock

Metamorphoses

The poplar's leaves turn, turning
    restless in no wind.
        The jays make war

on something young.
    Shrill mad cries!
        She shades her eyes,

helpless on the ground.
    Glaring heat at nine o'clock
        this July morning. . . .

What is given us,
    what is good?
        Seven decades of life

to vanish in an hour?
    She cannot say
        what her life has been,

who are her children,
    what wisdom drifts
        in her restless sleep.

She thinks:
    not all are transfigured,
        there are decent souls stuck

halfway,
    and suffering that is mute.
        What is given must be good,

but why do the jays scream?

She knows the night of her death
    will be like any other in the neighborhood,
        like any other.

The Demons

The newsprint blurs coyly.
The obituaries shift columns.

Salty fluid bites you—
the base of the spine
a rapid ascent
a geyser mean as mercury.
You cry: *Is this what I always was?*

No fear, there is always an exit.
Where the carpet is most soiled,
where your friends are jammed together
cheeks grazing cheeks
throaty chuckles like tiny drums.

A woman with your name
is counting sea-otters.
Above, the sun swerves too close.
It is not the Pacific, these white sands.
It is another time: the waters of the Gulf
        lap idly, idly.

If you betray the radiance of your being,
who will correct you?
There is no one else.
Temperatures melt, languid snows sigh,
the footprints of the dead are pressed down
in next spring's mud,
where you must walk.

Fearing demons you provoke them.
They fly in at all doors and windows, unbidden.
And the air is a scramble!—blinding, like chaff.
Better to welcome them:
face to face, one of you remains human.
Your weight balances the weight of those terrible limbs
        eager to spring into yours.

At the Seashore

the gulls' hysterical cries
the film-cool nerveless sun
the whimpering of a child dragged away
his father's muttering interrupted by the surf—
Tear you limb from limb—
as the man's strong bare toes clutch at the sand
and the child runs to keep pace
I swear I'll kill you one of these—

strangers are alarmed
within earshot
they exchange embarrassed looks—
Do you think—
should we—
should someone—
not sure what to do, whether—

situations change like the Atlantic sky
like the sand blown into peculiar angles
two rainstorms in a single afternoon
and now the gulls' familiar cries
now the cool pale sun
I swear I'll—
now the waves upon waves breaking loudly
cleanly
and there are hundreds of footprints
hundreds of ghost-shouts
murmurs
situations shift like sand
the sun will turn opaque and then burst forth again
and again
strangers will be embarrassed
will not know where to look, or whether
to look,
or why
a dog's quivering wail is a heartbreak
no lovers could long endure

After Sunset

Broken walls of waves
said to be the Atlantic
sweep toward us

Wave upon wave
so much is breaking
so much is happening

For centuries, here,
so much has happened
unrecorded
irretrievable

Droplets of water
bubbles of bright flesh
we stand here
hypnotized
again and always
and once again, again,
hypnotized out of flesh
jarred by the earthquake
of the sea

We are waiting
for something

We are waiting
for something to record

How icy the shock on our bare feet!

      A hundred yards away a vendor sells
      stickers for the bumpers of cars:
      the proclamation of the achievement
      of the replication of—
      The recording of—

We are waiting
again and always
and again, again,
stalkers of meaning
human and cold

Guilt

There was a steep hill there was stubbly snow
there was a creek filmed with white but not frozen
a child was saved from drowning there
a child's face was bruised against the ice there
they ran shouting to the creek bank they were angry
they waded in the thigh-deep icy water
they dragged the child out in stark heavy triumph

The small casket was closed it gleamed mother-of-pearl
the child lay motionless the child did not strike out
did not beat his fists against the handsome lid
the child had not drowned was not dead
they wiped false tears from their eyes
they winked at one another
their fingers were still raw from the ice
one of them had a cold his voice was hoarse
another's eyes were red-rimmed as if inflamed

In the cemetery the potted flowers are quickly overturned
boys run through the cemetery shouting
swinging whip-like willow branches
the flowers are overturned the clay pots broken
that is nature
that is only natural

When a child is saved from drowning beneath the ice
you cannot recall: was it you or another?
there are so many children
there are so many weed-stubbled snowy hills
cow pastures used for sledding
there are so many gasping struggles
you are too young your feet kick too frantically
you cannot possibly drown
you scramble for the bank and are hauled out dripping
wrapped in an adult's coat
carried safely home

When a child is saved or left to drown
you cannot recall which child it is or whose
child is scrambling now to shore
his mind vanished like water sucked into a drain
then wrapped shuddering in an adult's coat and hurried home
while the small frantic head bobs mid-river
sinking   rising   again sinking sinking
beneath the shredded ice-blue horizon

Abandoned Airfield, 1977

for my father, Frederick

In grass the cinder runways are hidden:
in grasses taller than children.
Nothing springs into movement but there is motion
      on all sides—
the shadows of low-flying planes
thinning to the shadows of starlings—
the trembling of pollen, the iridescence of black flies.
Above the corrugated roof a wind-sock flutters
      in gray shreds.
Thirty years. Thirty-five years.

Today's winds come from all directions.

Though it is Sunday there are no piper cubs circling
      to land,
there are no cars parked in the lot,
there are no children screaming with excitement
as their fathers test the sky.
The day's flying is over. It is nearly dusk.
The lightweight planes have dipped and soared and plunged
and fallen and righted themselves and risen and skimmed
low over that line of willows by the creek:
they have prepared soberly to land to taxi along the runway
to slow to come to rest to lie in broken rusted hulks.
The air-field is empty. The pilots sleep.
Exhausted, they feel the winds blow over them,
the grasses waving languidly above their heads.

Strange children have broken into the hangar,
have wrenched a door off its hinges.
Strange to us, the smears of tar and the smashed glass
and the small droning winds.
Who are we to survive those clumsy flights?
To recall the jarring thud of the plane's wheels
and the rightness of the cindery earth
and the sunburnt alarm of children who must witness
their fathers riding the air,
garish and frail as kites?

Now the field belongs to starlings.
Irritated by our presence they rise squawking
where gravity tosses them
and we cannot follow.

III

The Resurrection of the Dead

If You Must Go and I Must Stay

in waiting we are all alike
in the mind identical
in the art-work of waiting

"in a short while"
and then it is a wait
glacial
fluorescent-humming
as you fight to undrown
and I fight the panic of waiting
in the serious unmythologized
space
of a dozen squares of tile

the nurses' starched caps exclaim
a universe of small perfections
no rituals work here, only mechanics
where returning from the dead
is on schedule, or behind schedule
"in a short while"

dialed-down, the chill of the operating room
is an absolute zero
outwaiting even panic
our bodies' best concentration
no ritual but habit
waiting
surviving

There Are Those Who Die

There are those who die and are shoved
from us   There are those who die and are
given new names   There are those who die
and their dried nests burnt   There are those
who die but never leave the house   There are
those who die but curl beside us yawning and warm
There are those who spring into our fingertips
who live on a butterfly's ingenious wings
whose shouts echo across the choppy river

There are those who die and are walking
with the sunlight across the room
There are those who die and are exiled
those who are held aloft in cages
those who scuttle with rats
those dragged from the harbor faceless
those whose unprotesting veins are opened

There are those who die but send messages
shredded and rainstained
held trembling in someone's hand

Pretty Death

It will probably not happen today, you think.
Running a finger around the window frame,
measuring the dreamy raw sky—
it's been noon here, after all,
for quite a while

Razor-thin shadows & seed of chicory,
pray for us.

Those cries—? Children at play.
Children at their eternal play.
They play at rage, they play at pain.
They scream with laughter that never wounds.
They fall and scramble to their feet again,
alive.
They never bruise.

Moths & dandelions & child-fuzz,
pray for us.

It will probably not happen today.
The noon is too large.
The children are gigantic.
Here, behind the window, words cavort
in their difficult spaces.
It is now, it is always.
They fall and spring to life again
if only someone listens!
—But words drop first of all
with the brain's sudden stop.

Soul of muskmelons, sweet-scented seed,
pray for us.

Still, it will probably not happen today.
The sky is a famous fierce blue,
young squirrels scuttle in the eaves.
The children's faces are high-blown painted kites.

The Suicide

didn't thank
didn't wave goodbye
didn't flutter the air with kisses
a mound of gifts unwrapped
bed unmade
no appetite

always elsewhere

though it was raining elsewhere
though strangers peopled the streets
though we at home slaved and
baked and wept and
hung ornaments
and perfumed the dark
did he marvel
did he thank

was he grateful   did he know
was he human
was he there

always elsewhere:
didn't thank
didn't kiss
toothbrush stiffened with unuse
puppy whining in the hall
car battery dead
sweaters unraveled

was that human?

Went where?

The Broken Man

"What time did it happen—"
is one of their questions
strangers' faces form and unform
mumbling over what is done

what has passed by:
the Fifth Precinct and Mt. Carmel
Emergency and nurses quick
as children

He will not recall the terror
the hour of bleeding
the cars and trucks hurtling past
the pavement vibrating as if alive

O he will not recall
the death-pinch
the crossing-over
the giving-up

Icily his mind functioned
caught by a thread to his broken body
"What seems to be real . . . is not
always real"

He will not recall the rescue
that came too late

Now a soprano's voice rises suddenly
from a Schoenberg quartet
beside the tinfoil chrysanthemums
bodiless in beauty
beyond the spicy shame of blood
beyond hurt
and the memory of hurt

Enigma

I don't wish, she said,
to be merely filtered through.

Nor do I, he said.

Therefore they composed
songs of love:
they evoked granite-dark
theologies.

In public places they kissed.
Audiences sprang into being
to define their love.

Need it be said
they filled the sky?
His legs bestrid the ocean,
Her beauty glowed moon-pale.

Have we our wish, they wondered,
and I, overhearing, felt only pain
at their being filtered
through me now:
drop by drop by drop.

Ice Age

The Spirit moves where it will:
the air is scimitars, the air is shrieks.

All night the flesh of trees cracks
and in the morning the eye can gauge no distance,
the ear is deafened in white.

A world of glass!—many-winged glare of ice.
If the pulse beats it must learn caution
for here the slightest touch kills.

Razor-cruel is the light from the east.
We walk in blinded circles, helpless.
Trees—grass—stones—river—our steaming breaths:
the ice-drowse is upon us, the hypnosis
of ancient sleep.

In the Ice Age beauty fits tight as a mask of skin.
One cannot breathe, one stiffens to perfection.

Coronary Thrombosis

The rowboat drifts downriver.
The oars are raised and do not touch the water.
No noise, no strain.   . . . The old man drifts
downriver, a dark thread behind him
tightening.

Cast out, unreeled
in: the thread tightens smartly
and snaps.
Whistles are blowing—must be five o'clock.

Is that someone's grandfather who drifts by,
white hair hidden by a son's golfing cap?
No, it is an old man drifting in a rowboat
whose oars are locked in,
high from the water.
Soundless, his passage.
It is the peace our river ordinarily offers.

Preventing the Death of the Brain

Breathe.
    Breathe.

It is the body's angry imperative.
It is the first commandment.

Otherwise they will fade:
      the snowy sandstone of Mt. Invemere
      the mountain bluebells
      the screaming iridescent birds.
Otherwise they will go out.

You must breathe to keep them whole:
you must breathe to outpace your heart.

Fitted to the face is a transparent plastic mask.
Be careful not to twist the plastic tubing:
otherwise the oxygen will not flow,
otherwise the world will blacken and go out.

Clear odorless non-toxic
semi-soft resilient anatomically crafted to fit
most facial contours:
103 liters of oxygen
a precious green tank like a fire extinguisher
no one knows how to operate.

Gradually the brain responds, the eyeballs steady.
Gradually the trembling organism takes hold.
Oxygen is tasteless; there is no taste
but a brackish-dark puddle at the rear of the mouth.
A shadow that someday must be swallowed whole.

Emergencies are for strangers?
Yes.
And you are estranged from yourself,
now breathing and grateful and alive.
Emergencies are savage poems that elude the rhythms
we have devised.

Rumpled Bed

for Betsey Hansell

In these ruins a delicate light prevails
moon-blue
the dented shadows of dunes
hunch cruelly, and ravines drop
like the day sliding slowly under

In this mountainous terrain
cloth hurts like rock
abysses the width of a hair
open yawning and chill

Wrinkles in sheets sinuous as cracks
time itself rumpled, in bliss
of ice-blue hills and gulches and skies:
no human memory, here

      We fear such terrains
for they seize us mute
in these ruins of lumpy cold
where a single eyelash is razor-sharp
and look!—an eye in a stone face stares enormous

No words no words no words
a beginning and a probable end
a bassinet   a death-bed
shadow-soiled, fold upon fold of worn sheets
waves washing eternal
a planet's slumbrous play

The Resurrection of the Dead

Again now the flood   the first uproar
now they are returning
howling
this June morning that rings icy rain

The earth was water in these parts
long before its small continents rose
to day
now they reclaim it for the dark   for their own
clayey-red waves they are riding
shrieks of a river rising by minutes
by hours washing over the bridge
washing away the bridge, in screaming parts
the river a new countryside of motion
we have never seen before

The Childwold Cemetery breaks free at last   erupts
flings its fieldstone walls wide
the dead are lifted from their muddy sleep
awakened, the dead join the frolic of logs, broken birds,
soft-furred swimming shapes in the road

No maps now, no topography
no throats open to simple human song
the ditches swell babbling to creeks
the creeks swell to rivers
rivers to furious seas
propelling the dead who cannot be stopped
jubilant now on their Sabbath
chanting beating droning
careening against the low-hanging clouds
a wistful anger in their gestures
the ragged dead   the vengeful dead
our dead

no blood to them now, and eyeless,
briar-ripped, but brave
in roads   in ditches   in fields

hands missing
fingers, waving
fluttering still
in shallow water
a blast of odors
raw, playful
the aged, the
infants, the
mothers, the
uncles, broken
children, com-
panion now to
snakes, muskrats,
raccoons, birds,
wind-tortured
debris

I
am here

I
have
returned

I
want
my place
again

on
earth

the earth was
theirs long before
it was divided
into ours
now they rise
to reclaim it, now
they rise to reclaim
us
something jams itself,
look!—between the silo
and the barn—look!—
and when the winds die,
when the waves subside,
what calls to us, under-
growth about it like a shroud?

IV

Public Outcry

Happy Birthday

What a celebration, they shouted.
All afternoon, all evening, all night.
How generous. Who is giving us so much. Lovely,

to be unblushing,
stammering
      Someone cares for us after all!

Executive actions—mandates—crises are clattering
late into the night,
fluorescent lighting on all 56 floors
can be viewed all night long.
What a sacrifice, the witnesses are shouting.
Who is doing this for us, for us,
who imagines we are worth it, we
worth the labor of the mighty?

What point pessimism, the people who live in commercials
cry, what have you contributed to the economy anyway?
Next week's magazines are outdated.
Lead deposits sink to the bottom of water glasses
and can be easily spooned out.

What a celebration.
Who would choose to miss it, to sit hunched
in a corner, arms protecting his tender neck?
Sacrifices are winding their ways through city streets
common citizens are moved to public tears
many will be given free prizes
many will see their pictures in the paper—
who would resist the chanting,
who would refuse to open his veins?

Public Outcry

The Press displayed in three-inch red banners
the true story of the Governor's daughter's elopement
for weeks furies rage in the columns
H.W. of Redford Village is shocked
J.T. of Algonquin Township is not surprised
P.L.D. of Flint River Road is disgusted

There are traitors
there are amnesties
there are conspirators
there are celebrations releasing Birthday Balloons
there is a cardboard model of the President's log cabin
there is no penalty if it is set afire
except on the Sabbath

The Press invites public expression
the State Department balloons are there to be popped
jovial animal spirits are encouraged in a free society
as are meaningful relationships
Edenic connections
nostalgia by electronic miracle

> I telephoned a sixth grade classmate!
> I must have sounded anxious!
> Are you still there, all of you? I shouted
> across the miles
> What has Miss Connelly assigned for Monday?
> Am I in bad trouble? Can I catch up?

The Press is now publishing all the lottery winners
five red-star-bordered columns of electronic bingo winners
in small print the junior and senior high school winners
the crossword puzzle and 25-words-or-less winners
birthday people are urged to queue up at once
for free biopsies Monday Wednesday Friday mornings
those whose Social Security numbers begin with "2"
qualify this month for the Hawaiian Derby Sweepstakes
if the citizens should wish to boycott the Pentagon
if they should wish to frighten the Congress
they should refuse to turn on their faucets
each odd-numbered day of this month
they should write outraged letters to the Press
they should remember to sign their names

American Independence

Our balloon bodies float above the harbor
our fingers continue to pick at the empty red shells
grease-flecked, our large lips move
we are singing in near-unison
our thighs are enormous whitely-soft loaves of bread

"Why has this happened"
"What evil has been perpetrated upon us"
"Will no one have mercy"

Our skin is waffle-pocked
our fingers plump as breakfast sausage
our small eyes blink rapidly in our great faces
we carry souvenir lobster traps
one of us is vomiting into a Colonel Sanders bucket
"Why has this happened"
"Who is responsible"
we are waiting now for dinner

Patiently we turn the postcard racks
there are scoops of ice cream everywhere
gigantic yawns distort our faces
it is only 5:15
the day has been long
pistachio butternut raspberry coffee
New York strip steaks the red-boiled shells of dead creatures
tiny seals made of seal fur torn from living baby seals
"It is not our fault"

American flags float above the procession of cars
gulls dip and soar among us
doughy arms protrude from windows
fat knees are jammed up tight beneath chins
"Why is it so difficult to remain human"
we proclaim the American Independence
pancake batter clinging to our jowls
our stomachs test the resiliency of yellow stretch pants
oysters pulse a final spasm on our tongues
small curly dogs fret and yap and wet in our arms
"Let everything be ground down fine by our enormous jaws
by the heat of our tongues
let everything be transformed to human heat, human flesh,
human waste"

Immense with appetite we hurry to dinner
cockleshells and periwinkles and tiny moons are shattered
beneath our urgent shoes

Gala Power Blackout of New York City, July '77

"Allow me to assist you ladies," said a tall black moustached
youth to two burly black sisters struggling with an Ethan Allen
maplewood dresser upstairs in Coleman's Furniture of Harlem
while an elderly blind woman appeared wraith-like in the foyer
of the St. Regis Hotel to offer a candle to blackout victims
murmuring "You see, I won't be needing this" while at Brooklyn
General surgeons cheerfully operated by flashlight while the Met
performed all of Parsifal by torchlight to standing ovations
while fire hydrants gushed and residents of Gotham merrily soaped
and shampooed and squirted one another and romanced while Mrs.
Lucille Swann of the South Bronx returned her looted black-and-
white TV in exchange for a color TV (like her cousin Lucy Duck
of Detroit Michigan who did the same thing back in July 1967)
while marshmallows were roasted in the parks and cherry bombs
were ignited and there were free drinks at the GM Plaza and
romances in stairwells beneath gratings in subway cars in church
pews while "an almost festive atmosphere" prevailed by moon-
light and firelight twentyfive hours of camaraderie we're-all-in-
this-together an unidentified Puerto Rican youth climbed 107
floors on the outside of the World Trade Center to bring insulin
in a vial between gritted teeth to a stricken diabetic refused
a tip grinning immediately turned to descend the building "I might
be needed elsewhere" he said smiling while a bikini-clad gal
passed out Italian ices in Central Park and the radiation biology
labs of Columbia freed mice rats leghorns boas chimps in a moon-
lit bacchanal and the chorus of *Nude Thoroughbred Follies* high-
kicked along Broadway and Mr. Arthur Musgrave of Des Moines,
Iowa, collapsed in an epileptic fit at Lexington and 50th and
was not struck by car cab bus truck or delivery bicycle for forty-
five record minutes and democracy reigned at a champagne-caviar-
Quetzalcoatl-duck-paté-stuffed-wild-boar block party at Fifth
Avenue and 78th and the Angel of Washington Square Village
descended by helicopter to disperse martinis to stranded high-
rise victims and romances continued gaily in buses subways alleys
waterfront niches and stairwells and Don Barthelme sipped contem-
platively anisette on 11th Street by candlelight and by votive
light the B-minor Mass was performed at St. Patrick's for a
special audience of Mookes Island paraplegics and firemen in
Queens delivered a set of quintuplets by matchlight and an un-
identified passerby stopped gallantly to assist a woman who
turned out to be the visiting Queen of Iran "Allow me to aid
you lady as soon as I load up my own stuff" said the tall
softspoken black gentleman with a case of potted pheasant
beneath one arm and a case of Mary Cassatt Blackbird Rum
beneath the other.

The Noisy Sorrowful Ones

They cut their flesh into inch-long strips
they tottered above us on stilts
their eyes were black with pupil
their teeth were wetly white
their ecstasies soared to giggles
their pain stretched to yawns

It cannot be borne, they claimed
they seized us by the shoulders and claimed
to wish that we might be delivered
from the Garden like themselves
delivered soaring in ecstasy
transformed by bleating heedless breaths
they had wished to be aborted
were instead brought cruelly to birth
You cannot bear it either, they cry

stilted above us
smirking with wisdom
hot-breathed as if brotherly

You dare not bear it, they whisper
in baffled derision   in unison
ennobled now by granite and newsprint
lonely in posthumous pride

Revelations

Last night in a basement recreation room
there were people who refused to be recreated!
Husbands and wives who had surely met one another before
sat in stern silence side by side
staring at the faces opposite
staring at the simulated knotty-pine wall
and the wings of the Bird of Madness brushed near
and they did not notice
they did not even glance around!

I saw, I was there, I am the one.
They did not even glance around!

Last night it was revealed on the 11 o'clock news
that Western Civilization has been for the past fiscal year
held together by the stubborn courage of a chain-letter
originating in Saginaw, Michigan
consisting of thousands upon thousands
of good decent brave human beings
each certain he was the only winner
of the jackpot Million-Dollar Prize!

Tonight it will be revealed that the Bird of Madness
has flown overhead nightly   routinely
its wings flapping like laundry
its beak rusted at the tip
its eyes dull as old pennies
and only the united decency of the American people
and their refusal to incriminate the Creator
have kept things going as smoothly
as they've gone.

At Peace, at Rest

Stranded amiably on an island
of pavement by the drugstore
amid the crumpled wrappers and cigarette butts
in the 87 ° heat
there are three boys and two girls
sitting with their backs to the wall
arms linked loose about their knees
untalking
untroubled

In blue jeans and shapeless shirts
one boy in a purple jacket, unzipped
they sit hunched over their knees
blinking slowly in the sunshine
not talking
not waiting

The manager of the drugstore looks out
and ten minutes later looks out again
the children are peaceful they are no trouble
they are watching traffic
at noon they are watching traffic
at one o'clock they are still there
they are still there
another boy has joined them
fourteen years old and yawning and heavyheaded
halfsmiling at the traffic
he nudges one of the girls
they talk briefly they are old friends
they light cigarettes together
they stare at the traffic
they are silent

They are not waiting
they are not expecting anything
every holiday has arrived every package torn open
it is here, it is now
no trouble
at rest

Wealthy Lady

I am going to perform the rituals
of the body I woke up in
sweet insipid smiles writing
checks

I am writing writing powder
blue checks
I am prolific
I work best in the morning
though the 18th-century writing desk
of inlaid ivory
wobbles as I write
and I am distracted
by bugles and blood
the tapestry on the wall—
stags, hounds, horses,
red-garbed noble hunters—
scrambling through English briars
as I smile normal small smiles
and checks flutter blue
in all directions

I am performing the dream
I am performing the day
I am smiling sunshine into
an emaciated face in a photograph—
Korean or Vietnamese orphan—
I am smiling upon the Friends of the Symphony
the Committee to Conserve Our Forests
the Friends of the Art Institute
the Friends of the Mentally Handicapped
I have many adventures
I am smiling upon all races colors and creeds

When I begin to yawn and my hand is tired
I will leaf through the portfolio
someone keeps locked in the safe
I will finger the actual sacred papers
I will study the semi-annual statements
I will frown at the investment house's reports
but suppose all is well
I will fit to my small cool palm
the pistol someone keeps in the safe

I will hide it in my clothes
I will pace excitedly about the room
I will hurry to my luncheon appointment

no, I will go early to the gallery auction
at 10 there is the Van Dusen estate
a possible Goya a possible Rembrandt
or is it Van Gogh—
I will bid gaily and drunkenly and then
when the auctioneer is exhausted
when the gallery officers approach me
then I will

no, I will buy the cemetery north of town
I will turn it into a lush meadow
I want sheep grazing and rail fences and inner-city children
I want mists that linger till mid-morning
cow-bells and vespers and shepherds with staves
Lombardy poplars for the evening breeze
if the sheep get too filthy
if the children are vicious
if one of them approaches me

no, I will donate my glass harmonica
to the School for the Blind
I will write a check for the grape pickers
I will smile upon the Friends of Gaelic

at the club buffet I will toss rejected food to the floor
in a pique
I will look upon my lifelong friends without recognition
I will smile as they say *Won't you come with us . . . ?*
I will smile steadily as they approach me

no, I will park the car by a warehouse
I will go stumbling through the alleys
I will turn my ankle and whimper
when one of them approaches me I will run
I will be terrified
I will be panting like a doe
when one of them touches me
I will draw out the gun in triumph
I will cry *You thought I was a defenseless white woman . . . !*

I will remain at the ivory desk
already it is afternoon
the day will flutter by safely
powder blue smiles everywhere
but I intend to cross off my list
the Committee for the Preservation of St. Timothy's
it is headed by a swine who chews
celery
noisily

He Traveled by Jet First Class to Tangier

He traveled by jet first class to Tangier
where they had promised unusual sights
exotic strangers with date-dark date-soft eyes
sinewy dark limbs and flies swarming about beggars' stumps
he was mildly excited but not overcome
he was mildly intrigued scribbling impressions in his notebook
he took snapshots he bought perfume he hired a guide
he traveled by jet first class to the Arctic
where they had promised unusual sights
he took snapshots of the Northern Lights he gathered fossil rock
he was friendly with the U.S. Army Engineers
he scribbled impressions in his notebook of the mountains
of chunky blue ice of the ravenous sea-birds of the Eskimos
he took a snapshot of a polar bear but it was an ice chunk
he traveled by jet first class to Sydney
where they had promised unusual sights
he took snapshots he recorded impressions he rented a car
he saw the aborigines he bought clay pots he made friends
they were talking about Rio
he had been in '67
he had a notebook filled with Rio
he had Kodak color film from that trip still undeveloped
he felt a pleasant melancholy sometimes
it was a genuine human feeling
he flew by jet first class to Inverness
he stayed in a quaint 16th-century inn
it was cold as the Arctic there were northern lights
he took photographs of a ruined church he took photographs
of the mountains as the sun set he changed his plans
flew to Barcelona had to switch planes in Lisbon switched
by accident to a Rome-bound plane scribbled impressions
high above Florence in a blizzard was forced to land in Munich
he had been in Munich once he refused to leave the plane
he flew impulsively to Tokyo he scribbled impressions
he took snapshots of the smog he interviewed a Hiroshima survivor
he flew to O'Hare he liked O'Hare he liked the Cattleman's T-Bone
he liked the Tropicana Revolving Drum Bar he flew to Death Valley
he explored the desert collected fossil rock picked cactus flowers
found himself in Tangier refused to leave the plane flew to Wales
recorded his melancholy observations found them succinct
found them lyric and legitimate and authentic human truth

he traveled by jet first class to Oslo there were northern lights
he flew slantwise across India stayed overnight in Hong Kong
switched planes in Madrid lost his appetite for spicy food
reserved a top-floor suite at the finest hotel in Paris
told himself it was all quite remarkable quite genuine
I am only human he thought this is proof I am normal
we are all normal he thought how could we be otherwise
he booked passage to White Dwarf he felt vertiginous he felt better
in Whippletree South Dakota he regained his appetite he bought film
he traveled by jet first class to Gulf of Anadyr for the mating
of the whales he took snapshots he recorded impressions he flew
to New York City for the Royal Ballet to Tasmania to the Calgary
Stampede to Dublin to Venice to Ta, South Korea to the Oder Hilton
to the Baltic Cruise a stop-over at Le Havre appetite improved
ivory and opal trinkets at the Nigerian festival handwoven straw
hats and sandals at the Prawn Festival at Oahu a new island
discovered northeast of Brazil Fernando de Noronha it was unspoiled
he booked a top-floor suite overlooking the bay lost his camera
was bored at the Gulf of Guinea recording his impressions
melancholy human truths accepted makeshift accommodations in Panama
wept soundlessly on the Aegean rallied in New Zealand in the sun
summarized his notebook in Ceylon began another vertigo intriguing
loss of appetite intriguing in New Orleans for the Mardi Gras
he was philosophical in Budapest he was cheerful in Dahomey
he was depressed in the Ardennes then again in Luxembourg
felt quite fine in Göteborg began to see the pattern of things
in Napa then quite clearly in Peloponnesus lost the thread
in Nanga Parbat subdued but philosophical in Afghanistan
loss of appetite insomnia fatigue lyric human melancholy
he rallied in Iceland he was normal in Jutland a stop-over in Athens
did the trick he bought another notebook he bought film
all quite normal he thought everything is normal he thought
all quite human he thought
how could we be otherwise?

V

Many Are Called

The Creation

A lightning-stroke,
    and we appear.
A lightning-stroke,
    and we appear to each other.

A commandment on a mossy rock:
Live as if you were immortal.
Then the counter-signs, the cautionary
Beware—
        every pore is a betrayal—
           all flesh is grass, and the goodliness thereof—

A lightning-stroke,
    and the world is ridged with shadows.
Perfect, are we? In love?
We quarrel to regain our souls.

Not-being

Not-being is a sort of being, Plato says slyly.
And yet one who almost died returned to say
there is no gravity there.

It is perfect union: no consciousness.
It is your face pressed flat against
your mirrored face.
Blind, perfect, without perception.
Not even your shivering will prevail.

If we ease into one another,
how can I love you?
If our pseudonyms must be surrendered,
won't we swim through bits of ourselves,
scattered everywhere?

The troubled skies will be one sky,
the mind's head-hammering will subside,
it will be revealed that suicide
is an impossibility.

Shape-Changers assume the guise
of relatives and old friends.
They neither lie nor tell the truth
but inform you, slyly, like the poets:
Being is a sort of non-being already.
And why are you afraid? It is only yourself.

Love Poem

Taking the curve of the road too fast
the car swerves, tires hit gravel,
fence posts never seen before lurch crazily
then are righted again.
A miracle.
Our pulses now race in a single spasm:
other curves lie ahead.
If we die today we die together.

That

        single pear in its ripeness
this morning swollen-ripe
its texture rough, rouged

more demanding upon the eye than the tree
branching about it
more demanding than the ornate drooping limbs
of a hundred perfect trees

yet flawed: marked as with a fingernail
a bird's jabbing beak
the bruise of rot
benign as a birthmark
a family blemish

still, its solitary stubborn weight is a bugle
a summoning of brass
the pride of it subdues the orchard
more astonishing than the acres of trees
the army of ladders
the workers' stray shouts

        that first pear's weight
exceeds the season's tonnage
costly beyond estimation
a prize, a riddle
a feast

An Infant's Song

And then I was imagined into life:
chance could not have determined that plunging
of blood into blood,
or the coalescing of straw-hued fluid
into something so tough—
who could have mistaken my shape beneath the river's surface
though water has lost its transparency in this age?

Everywhere are sisters and brothers
emerging shyly, fiercely, in the good weather
of homes with basements and storm windows
and the 11:00 news—
What if the current that bore Keats warmly to his burial
bore our parents to their first astonishment?
—or to a sky of blackbirds with red-flashing wings
                pumping the air to ecstasy?

We emerged, we are here.
We begin now the effort of imagination:
to reconstruct how an eye-blink, an instant's crack of light,
made wild the familiar back yard
the over-known property
the contracted marriage
every pattern of the world's invisible currents,
somehow no longer enough.

In Medias Res

Arriving at the midpoint of your life
and finding it a café in West Virginia—
drafty, smelling of grease, with mud-stained floor—
what better ritual, than to unlearn irony
and wash your hands?
If you flee, the sky will break into sleet.

There have been warnings all along, and friendly curses.
You can do nothing right.
You can do nothing wrong.
No virtues are permitted you,
and no crimes.

Arriving at the midpoint of your life
and finding it a café in West Virginia—
what strategy more proper, than to shrink to the size
of a matchbook's soiled cover?
Caution. Close before striking.
Contract to a few inches' square teasing
of another traveler's eye.

Earth-Rituals

> Earth, give me roots!
> —Timon of Athens

tendrils tough as muscle pry, seek, poke
into the lead pipes
fathoms beneath the house
in dizzying oceanic silence

their quarrels lack brutality
because they are silent
for decades, for centuries, they pry and seek
probable pathways, they poke into one another
by accident
yet in perfect union:
as a dreamer wisely embraces his dream

the thunderous staccato of rain
the blaring of maddened red sirens
the bombs whose noise cannot be registered
the birds' interwoven cries—
are muffled in earth
in that shadowless silence
where nothing registers
and the dreamer may spin
unknowing through parts of himself:
former lives, future lives, prying into
the lives of others, his dream-images innocent
as roots,
no boundaries
no rituals
no obvious struggles

except the occasional heaving of the earth
the realignment of what had been permanent

Fertilizing the Continent

Fluid as music we pass through,
and return, bringing ancestors
to this new place:
our childhood bones merging, melting.
The map's divisions snarl, breaking
as we pass effortlessly through.

The continent takes us on
begins to dream us:
worlds shading into worlds.
What integrity in our bones' fated structure?—
the right language dispels it.

Rituals seek to enter us
as if the body were a sacred event.

Many Are Called

The great tide of noon!—and a flood
of voices, unchorused.
Thistles regain their pollen.
Junked autos heave from ditches.

Unwary in opposition
we pass too close to each other—
we are drawn together—
voiceless, we disappear
into each other.
It is August: in a creekbed, an enormous boulder
greens and richens with slime.

Our omens were always correct.
Our interpretations were faulty.
And our farewells?—premature.
It seems that all are chosen.